Praise for

Songs for Ghosts

Julie Valin's poems in *Songs for Ghosts* are that crackle and pop of the needle hitting the record, the first sliver of moonshine through the window, the thump in the chest when love calls, the sound of a radio on in an empty room, and the songs you choose to play when ghosts appear. There is a deep rhythm to these poems. They are that 1980s first synthesizer kiss, the alternative circa 1991 combat boot kick in the heart, the razor wire of punk that leaves scars to be proud of, and they soothe and sin like the blues.

–Todd Cirillo, *Kisses From a Straight Razor*, Six Ft. Swells Press Publisher

Julie Valin is a poet of barrooms and jukeboxes, buttercups and bird ghosts, snapshots and lazy angels. In her collection, *Songs for Ghosts*, she takes her reader on a vivid ride, filled with music and sunlight, nostalgia and hope. She tells the reader, "All the poets have already said it the right way," but that doesn't stop Valin from saying it her way. The poems offer the reader a dynamic, honest, melodic adventure, in a world where she lets us know from the beginning, "I am the radio left on in an empty room." Valin's affection for the connection between music and memory are an ongoing theme, playing throughout her poems. It's as if the reader is sitting beside her when she writes, "...I go back to the Blues, / sip my coffee / with a splash of bourbon, / watch the record spin behind the glass, / and listen to poets sing / 80-year-old words / to fill me up / once again." This is an invitation to pull up a barstool and pore over the dazzling *Songs for Ghosts*.

–Kirsten Casey, *Ex Vivo: Out of the Living Body*, Poet Laureate of Nevada County, CA

I don't know what that *thing* is . . . that thing that makes a poem great, but whatever it is, Julie Valin has got it. She writes of ghosts, record players, and the romance of cheap beers—

of things lost and the sensuality of everyday moments—every word a frayed yet somehow perfect translation of the endless longings of the heart. Like an old master blues picker, she plays the truth in every note, and lifts our spirits to the moon.

–Shawn Odyssey, Edgar and Agatha Nominated author of *The Oona Crate Mystery* series

The poetry of Julie Valin's *Songs for Ghosts* is immediately accessible and engaging, alive with music and precise imagery. These poems are full of the stuff of life; the big passions as well as the quiet moments that reveal our common humanity. Simultaneously playful and full of hard-won insight, this collection maps the human condition with the truth and humor of Valin's unique voice.

–William Taylor Jr., *Pretty Things to Say*

In *Songs for Ghosts*, Julie Valin's rhythmic, addictive voice pays tribute to life's sublime, beautiful, and hauntingly painful details—it sings!

–Kim Culbertson, *Songs for a Teenage Nomad* and *Catch a Falling Star*

Julie Valin's poetry is a delight: amusing, heartfelt, thought-provoking. Valin infuses many of her poems with her love of music; readers feel as though they are with her, driving down the road, crooning along to the radio. In Playin' the Storm Out, she writes, "My own blues, / my own flat notes and rises: / a song in the windchimes, / the sad and hopeful harmonica / of my memory / never taken out and played." In this collection, Valin captures that sense of ineffable longing most of us have felt at some time, though have not been able to give voice to. For all of what life encompasses, read *Songs for Ghosts*.

–Judie Rae, *The Weight of Roses* and *Howling Down the Moon*

SONGS FOR GHOSTS

Songs for Ghosts

Julie Valin

Meadowlark
PRESS
Emporia, Kansas, USA

Meadowlark Press, LLC
meadowlarkbookstore.com
meadowlarkpoetrypress.com
P.O. Box 333, Emporia, KS 66801

Songs for Ghosts
Copyright © Julie Valin, 2022

Cover Design: Julie Valin, Self to Shelf Publishing Services

Interior Design: Linzi Garcia, Meadowlark Press

Author Photo: Julie Valin

Ghost Boy Illustration: Kate Smith

POETRY / American / General
POETRY / Subjects & Themes / General
POETRY / Subjects & Themes / Places

ISBN: 978-1-956578-10-2
Library of Congress Control Number: 2022935150

For Todd Cirillo,
who always listens to my songs
regardless of which ghosts are around.

Playlist

Empty Room Radio

You are my favorite song
that hasn't come on in years,
the one I dance in the car to,
or play while chopping onions
with the steady beat
and a wild trumpet solo.

I am Nina Simone, beckoning:
Do I move you,
are you willin'?
Do I groove you, is it thrillin'?

I am BB's Lucille,
my soul strummed and bent,
ringing out, filling every corner
of the space you stand in,
long after
I've walked away.

I am 3 a.m. blues,
Koko Taylor's Voodoo Woman,
I can look through water, and spy dry land.
I'm looking through water now, and
can still make out your face.
I swear,
you're smiling.

I am the radio left on
in an empty room,
my hopeful notes
plucking the curtains
with the kiss of a harmonica,
a chorus of pleas.

Owl Ink

The attention to detail
he gives to my back
is so painstaking, it buzzes.
My shoulder blades
are the most sensitive;
I flinch when he traces
the wings.
The moon hangs
in the center, cool
midnight blue.
The eyes: two Mexican pinwheels
of orange and purple.
Red bleeds
the most, dotting
my spine in tears
of feathers.
The branch
of my grandmother's initials
holds it all up—
as it always will—
until it's just
a part of my bones.

Julie Valin

Anywhere but Here
for Todd

He laid 800 miles down
on his set of wheels
one song at a time.
A pirate in a black truck
raiding nature
of its adventure
on the side of the road.
That sunset over the Pacific—
pure gold
he pillaged on his phone camera
after a long, hard night
of killing traffic.
When he got to where
it satisfied him,
      anywhere but here,
the beach was spread
before him
like a welcome mat
where he left his boots.
The local tavern
served cold ones
and fried calamari
with pretty, small-town waitresses
who listened to stories of his travels,
hoped he'd stay long enough
to become part of one.
But he was off again
too quickly,
the girls not able to compete
with his love
of the smooth curve
of the steering wheel,
the whisper of the tires on the road,

the kiss of mile markers blowing by,
and his only muse—
the complete,
gratifying
feeling
of speeding toward
anywhere
but here.

Barbie (ill)Logic

I remember no matter what top I put on Barbie—
whether a blouse or a knit sweater—
her boobs were so prominent, like two
perfectly smooth mountains.
It's not that I liked them, or was envious of them,
I just didn't understand what their purpose was
except to distinguish her as a woman.
And sometimes it felt odd to be a little girl
playing with a woman doll who does grown-up
and womanly things.
Of course I made her ride in the convertible
with Ken, and I often made her and Ken kiss,
with Ken's stiff arms at her hips,
and her arms never able to wrap around
his neck like I'd seen in movies,
but up there
attempting it.
And since their plastic heads
were not able to tilt,
I had to slant their bodies
in a criss-cross,
so they could reach
each other's mouths.

Later, as I began
to do grown-up and womanly things,
in t-shirts or sweaters—
I almost felt like Barbie,
stiff and awkward,
and always that first kiss
with a permanent dumb
smile plastered
across my face.

Instructions on Not Writing

Talk about it all the time, how you're not writing. Act mad. Act like writing is a thing with fists to be mad at.

Listen to the regarded poet on the radio say that she can't manage to call herself a poet, because it's too lofty of a term. Think about that for the whole car ride home.

Think about how you so cavalierly call yourself a poet. Think about how you never really thought about its implications when you say it out loud to another person. How lofty it sounds.

Instead of staying up nights writing during the blue hour when the rest of the house is asleep—binge on all the episodes of Mr. Selfridge in a two-week time span. Go about your day with Mr. Grove on your mind, hoping he'll pull through. Or at least, have one last go-around with Josy.

Agree to your writer friend that you will write 600 words by Friday to send to her, but then treat it like it's another college paper that you know you won't get to until 2 hours before midnight on Friday. Except you'll know it's not actually a college paper, so you really won't get to it until the following Tuesday.

At an attempt to save yourself, buy the audiobook Big Magic and listen to it on the drive to coach your student for a poetry competition. Be inspired for precisely 38 minutes and 6 traffic signals, and smile out the window to the rain. Know that your own Big Magic will come after hours and hours of dredging, but put off looking for where you last put the shovel because you'd rather watch another episode (or three) of Mr. Selfridge.

Forget the quote you had Siri write on your phone that said, "Artists by nature are gamblers," because the only thing you're good at gambling away is all the time you've spent not writing.

Look at the clock. It's 11:18 p.m. Your eyes are squinting at the computer screen and your husband is snoring in bed. There is nothing romantic about this. But you notice that the click of the keys makes some kind of new music that intermingles with the rain clicking the roof. Know there is nothing romantic about this.

But the keys are tapping out steps. Keep rolling.

Playing Chicken

We were neck-and-neck—
double lanes on the highway,
he in his red pickup,
me in my grey 4-door,
for 1, 2, 3, maybe 6 miles
together,
pushing our luck,
72, 78, 84 MPH.
Turning his head,
he smiled at me
then veered off
on an exit
in the middle of nowhere,
not having the guts
to take it any further.

Julie Valin

Kiss

When it finally happens
it's a tingle of new blood
on the tip of your tongue,
a pinpoint,
a precise moment
frozen hot—
singed like an old photograph.
The quiet light
behind your eyes
melting red,
your fingertips
alive in awareness,
the soft flesh inside
your mouth
stirring.
       Everything—
your whole life,
those missed dances,
the glances sent
elsewhere,
the lone walks home,
the third wheels,
the silent phones,
the misplaced compliments,
      it all blows away
      in ashes,
until all you know in this world,
is this long lick of flame—
its blue center
that burns the hottest
      when his lips
      finally find
      their way
      to yours.

Ghost Writing

Losing you is like having a phantom limb—
the creative arm of my body
torn away   so swiftly
that I was still in the middle
of saying goodbye
before I realized
it was no longer
my hand
that was waving.

It's difficult now,
finding other ways to move
through my days
on a path
that will never wind back
to our Thursday lunches
at Pine St. Café
working through poems,
or our after-hours gatherings
at the corner bar
where our quarters
ruled the night.

Now it is my own hand
that moves the pen across the page,
with only the memory
of your arm
swatting at gnats
to let inspiration
swirl freely
around me.

Julie Valin

I will do anything—
hurl liquor bottles against the wall,
throw punches at drunk guys in alleys—
anything
to create my own scenes
to write about,
but the truth is,
maybe I'll just have to settle
for reading your poems
written about other bars and alleys
in a more colorful place
far from this small town,
and let how much that haunts me
serve as the best inspiration
I'm going to get.

Buttercup

Buttercups, their little faces.
If you hold one up to your chin,
and it glows, my nana said,
then you are boy crazy.

Mine never *didn't* glow.

Those beautiful weeds.
It's hard to pick them,
unless you're making a bouquet
for a frog,
I tell my daughter,
her petal-soft fingers
pinching the small stems
as she arranges a cluster
to offer me,
unaware
of how many frogs
she will go through,
unaware of how golden
they cast a glow
before she hands
them
to me.

Julie Valin

Sister Seeds

My sister said in her
Maid of Honor speech
to her best friend,
that she is like a sister
to her—she smiled—
sometimes better
than a sister,
she added.
I gulped
my champagne.
Pins stung
the back of my throat
all the way down.

I am her only sister.

We are two flowers
sprung from sister seeds.
We flourish in the same soil,
grow side by side, shoots
holding hands, reaching up
to the same sun.
Our stems mark
our memories as spines do.
When I blossom,
she blossoms.

        Little sister,
now I have been plucked

and set in a vase.

A Lá Cinema Paradiso

He stood below her window
every day for 30 days.
Even in the downpour,
his eyes were lit up
with the sun of hope.
His shoulders never slouched
with waiting. The drops
rolled around his form
like he was the statue of David.
At a time when boys kissing girls
in American movies was snipped out,
he was the film uncoiled
from the floor, vigilantly spliced
into the ending scene when the camera
zooms into focus on her window,
the curtain gliding open
like a stormdoor swung out wide
into the wild streets,
and every clutch and kiss
ever desired and remembered
floods from one heart to another.
And him, unwavering, lets it
swell over him,
because he is young
and eager to dive deep
into the dark waters
of love.

By the end,
we have all reeled
our hearts on the screen—
I am neither the girl
behind the window

or the boy in the rain,
but the unspooled film
waiting to be salvaged
and threaded through.
All it will take is someone
with a still-curious heart
to pick it up off the floor,
to play out the ache
and desire
it took to create
those scenes,
and stick around
long after the credits roll.

Endless Tomorrows

*"you were right about the stars –
each one is a setting sun."*
—Wilco

How many times I've watched the light play on your face that way
half in, half out—
bars of shadow and day breaking
over bedsheets,
the 5 a.m. hour tugging you away,
shackled to the sun's
burning call. You stir and bend
in the opposite direction
from where my light wakes.

You move through your days
as golden light
you wear on your skin,
pine needles and sweat,
blackberries and creekbeds—
a breeze you carry
through the door
when you come home.

I am twilight,
hair tips dipped in indigo,
musk and promises,
red wine and silver-lined
dusk on porches,
I am a vista of endless tomorrows
rising to greet each
of your setting suns;

we are the red spark
on the horizon
from where you leave off
and I keep going.

Julie Valin

This Is the Color of What's Inside

*to the unknown flowering shrub on
the side of Auburn-Folsom Rd.*

Underneath the hardness,
the stark and the unbudging,
is this color of fuchsia, but
you have to leave everything behind
to find it. You have to listen
to your favorite podcast
about a man who risks everything—
including love—to jump off cliffs,
living his own metaphor
to the hilt.

You have to give it all up—
the roles you play in everyday life,
the dirty dishes, laundry,
grocery shopping, 532 unread emails—
all of it,
until you are back to your
bare minimum: the essentials,
the base of what makes you
one in a million; seeing
with a clear heart the beauty
that makes it beat again
to the music
only you hear.
This.
This is why you made that u-turn.
This is what will get you back
on the road,
humming.

When Ghosts Appear

for Carey Floyd, "Crazycloud"

He claimed he saw Bukowski,
the now long-dead poet,
who just appeared before him,
smiling big,
standing over a bird.

"A bluebird?" I asked cleverly,
referencing his most famous poem.
"No, just a regular bird," he replied matter-of-factly.
I was curious.
"I wonder why he was smiling?"
"I think he was trying to tell me
that things were going to be really good for me
from now on."
I wanted to press him.
"Why the bird?"
"Because the bird represents me,
how I travel from port to port
with not a thing to my name, and never
a need to unpack, just exploring any place
I want, away from the people."
"Hmm, that's cool," was all I could say.
"That's just my interpretation," he continued.
"When ghosts appear, you can't ask them
why they're there, you can only guess.
You can be right, or you can be wrong.
You'll never know for sure.
That's the thing about ghosts."

We were quiet for the rest of the car ride
home. He was looking out the window
at the swamp, at the Yucca trees,
at the crumbling stones

of the ancient Fort St. John.
He pointed out a lone bird
in the middle of the field
standing by an
unmarked grave,
foraging
for worms
as the green grass
waved.

Rebirth of the Cool

title stolen from Afghan Whigs, who stole it from Miles Davis

for W.S. Gainer

Out my café window,
the old man rounds the corner
in a brand new silver Honda Pilot.
He's wearing his trademark plaid button-down
but is a little more hunched over the wheel.
I watch him make the turn to downtown
and wonder where he's off to . . .
the bookstore to stock it up
with his latest free poetry book,
or the menswear store to look
for more plaid button-downs, or perhaps
a gift for his wife, something sweet.
As he drives off, his bumper sticker
winks at me:
Lebowski 2020.
Goddamn, I laugh out loud in the café,
the dude may be old
but a cloud of cool
still lurks in his long shadow.

Julie Valin

Moving Target

When you said you were going
to drive off a cliff
if I didn't stay with you,
I thought it was a romantic prospect.
I imagined you in your 280 Z,
a little silver bullet,
gunning up over the ridge
of Devil's Slide
where the edge of the earth,
and the Devil himself,
sit on the passenger side—
the seatbelts secured
just for irony's sake—
saying nevermind
the steering wheel.
The hood would strike the sun
like gunfire,
if you were aiming upward.
And I know your flaming determination
would at least saw off
part of a cloud.
But there's nothing spectacular
about eventually reaching your target,
especially when it's moving

away.

The Journey of a Song

It was born in my stuccoed living room
from a stacked stereo,
amp on the bottom,
record player on top,
wires stretching the room
connecting wood-paneled speakers.
It was born from a treasured collection,
seeping out like crystal-clear fog.
It was born in the colors blue and then red,
both cool and hot, leaving a burn either way.
The song was born a song, yes,
but it grew up to be
walks to the Mexican store after a hangover
to have *birria*,
the gravel popping under tires
the time I sped away,
the snaketurn road
of Devil's slide,
the moon smirking through the skylight,
the long goodbye
and the last kiss.

Then the song
set off on its own path,
found its freedom
in mellow backyard gatherings,
barrooms with jukeboxes.
It had its fun
in psychedelic escapades in the forest,
dreams of red houses on
green rolling meadows,
behind many cracked-open doors
in poster-walled bedrooms,

Julie Valin

in cars at midnight perched on high hills,
in the buttons of the blouse
of the girl
in your backseat.

When it came back
it was like that knock on the door
you see in movies
where the lieutenant tells you your son
has died bravely,
except no one has died,
exactly.   But something has.
The song arrives to tell you this
in an outdoor restaurant
near the blue shores of Lake Tahoe,
drinking your favorite Heffeweisen
and eating calamari
across from the one you love most,
and possibly, the one you have loved
all along, before you even met,
before the stuccoed living room
or in spite of it.
Yes, the song says,
something has died

in order
for
this
to live.

Stranded

After a tough day
of being a mom
with no other aspects
of me showing,
I am huddled
against the kitchen sink,
water running to drown out the sound
of my daughter crying
for something,
when all she ever gets
is my undivided love.

I pretend to wash
sippy cups, or the vegetables
I should be cooking for dinner,
but instead I reach in the freezer
behind the Eggo waffles,
tucked in there neatly,
slide out my bottle
of gin, sip
right from the lip.

On the other side of town,
friends gather and drink
cheap beer pitchers,
laugh and tell stories
of their days at the river
or their musical nights
with new and exciting strangers,
wonder where I am
for a brief moment.

Hopeless,
I retreat

Julie Valin

to the living room
where my daughter is now
coloring and quiet,
learning her letters.
I look down
and there, under her pink sea
and purple seahorses,
among the scribbles and squiggles,
the message is clear:
S . . . O . . . S

A Good Defense

When I was 16
the Tarot Card Lady
at the psychic fair
told me I was an armadillo.

"You have had bad things
happen to you," she said,
in that other-worldly voice
that psychics use that is whispery
and sounds like the strings of a sitar.

"So you have protected yourself," she went on,
"with your leathery armor shell."
If there was internet back then
I would have looked up on Wikipedia
what the hell armadillos are even made of,
or what animal family they're in,
but instead I just thought of how, strangely enough,
I did always love a good leather jacket . . .
and then I just nodded,
scrolling through my childhood.
I thought of all the kids on the playground
by the monkey bars, and Kari and Jan
skipping off to leave me alone in the woodchips;
or all those times my brother got to sit in the very
back of the station wagon to have the long window
all to himself; or how I always had to borrow Lisa's Jordache jeans
to replace my Mervyn's specials; or the time I shoved my sister
down on her twin bed and slapped her cute cheeks
while my dad's shape suddenly loomed in the doorframe;
or all those family dinners around the table
when my mom made me eat every bite of my spinach.
Realizing I always lived to fight another day,

Julie Valin

I sat up straighter in my seat.
"Yes," I said, looking into the Tarot Card Lady's eyes.
I'm a motherfucking armadillo. Just try to punch
through this, and you already know what will happen . . .
I strutted away, the studs
on my leather jacket
glinting.

Eye of the Moon

Moon: smile only if you mean it.
On the other side of the world
are you going around
doing the same thing?
I'm sure the angle is different there,
the shadows in the middle-
east showing prominently, your lit corners
turned down.

I know what your
Chesire blinks mean,
the way your smart pupil
dilates through our windows,
waxing your observations
in a density
that never wavers.
Craters form every time
someone wishes on you—
the gravity of it all
steadying your track.

They depend on you, you know.

The ones who crouch
in light-drained places,
throbbing from the cracks
they fell through,
looking up, waiting.
The ones who cry
for the sun to turn a new day,
for the sleepless night to die
another death.

And, boy, do you come for them
like a god.

But tonight I caught you,

 yellow moon,

 your tired eye

            closing

on all of us.

Strange Plants

The sun on my face
is a bright kiss,
so I linger in it.
I let it kaleidoscope colors
behind my eyes
until it turns pink
and then red.
The warmth is my meditation;
bird song, my spa music;
the far-off hornsound
of the small plane—
a promise.

I can't tell the difference
between my skin, my body,
my limbs—the rays of sun itself.
My wilted fingertips
bud velvet petals.

About this time of day,
you would be working
out in the field, stalking
through brush, making a path
in succinct map lines and points,
memorizing trees.
But I wonder,
do you remember
the words my skin calls forward,
the points where my curves
hold a place for you?

Julie Valin

We are all just strange plants,
and touch
is our sun.

You are my sun
and our silence
is clouds,

but when you come home,
I will open the curtains wide;
let it all
pour in.

"The Days Run Away Like Wild Horses"
title borrowed from Bukowski

and there is so much dust,
hooves on the wind
blowing my hair back with hot breath.

Art and nature at work:
the beautiful heaving of muscles
under the velvet fur.

I can only stand in one place.
Watch it all surge through.
Hold on to my daughter's hand.

Now she says goodbye
at the curb,
even that is moving away.

The house that still stands
holding snapshots in its packed-up walls—
lopes out of sight.

My uneven breath as I stand in the dust
in one place,
holding on to my hat.

The beautiful moving away
on longer legs with pink backpack,
the small last turn.

There is so much dust.
Goodbye waves on the wind.
I hold on to my hat.

Julie Valin

The Angel Pulls Some Strings

"The angels are sitting on their asses."
—Deborah Brass

Perhaps even the one that brought you and I
together. That one could amount to something
if she didn't think her job was done. She's been
having a perpetual spa day, watching reality TV,
sipping Chai lattes, staying away from carbs
except for the occasional potato chip . . .
anyway, she's sitting pretty, knowing
all the strings she pulled—that whole internet thing—him breaking
up with that dud girl—me having the epiphany that
drummers are too egocentric, etc. etc.—it was all calibrated
perfectly and was good, wholehearted work.
I'll give her that.

Then she sat up there in all her glory
on our wedding day, us posing for our photos
on the top of that large, flat boulder,
raised high above the parking lot and RVs
so the only backdrop was sky blue, blue sky—the kind
of blue that sets off fluffy white clouds
in a heavenly manner.
Then she laughed at her own joke
when the two red-shouldered hawks
came circling and arcing above us,
and I cried out in amazement,
"Look! There's our spirit birds!"
. . . but it turned out to really be
two turkey vultures
waiting for whatever
we would leave behind.

Our angel stuck around for a good stretch after.
Saw us off on a number of memorable
Mexico trips with the best *machaca* and *camárones*,

deals on silver jewelry, your best tans,
that cinnamon tequila, the burning sunsets
that lit our eyes in red-hued gold.

There were the poetry nights, too,
the jukebox nights with friends and
cheap beers and karaoke to Men Without Hats
and backyard parties with those blue
Elvis drinks. Nights in San Francisco,
just you and I, seeing live music
in small venues, the holiday lights in
Union Square for my birthday,
riding public transit
to the Pork Store on Haight
for our favorite breakfast. There were quiet
nights too, filled with nothing in particular
except the easy push of a comfortable life.

Her big feat was the gift of the sun
rising from a new room in our house.
I'm sure she cashed in a favor from the angel
who gets the stars ready each night,
probably to make up for the time
she left off the tail of the bull. Regardless,
I'm sure they had a field day after pulling
that off, and justified to themselves that
it was okay to slack off and eat a whole
bag of potato chips.

That goddammed angel
absolutely has to be retired now,
or she might have quit long ago
with no replacement. Not all angels

Julie Valin

have the best work ethic, and they
can get complacent when the hearts
that have been pierced by their arrows
have worn into just being pierced hearts.

All the angels are sitting on their asses
because we
are sitting on our asses.
It's that valley in our lives
that needs just common miracles
and we can only look to each other
for that.
The angel's free in that knowledge,
and I'm still looking
for a flutter
of her wing
to carry me through.

Playin' the Storm Out

The sky is dark and hovering low
and the cold steel wind
makes the bare branches wave
bye bye, baby, bye bye.

Everything's gone—
nothing to face what's brewing
except me and the sleeping dog,
and this old beer snuck
from the back of the fridge.

My own blues,
my own flat notes and rises:
a song in the windchimes.
The sad and hopeful harmonica
of my memory
never taken out and played,
now dusted off as the clouds beat
rain drops down,
my lips humming in its teeth,
singing,

Ain't nobody left me
but myself . . .
Ain't nobody left me
but myself.

Julie Valin

How to Come Back From the Dead

First, go through all the necessary channels
of dying: seeing the light, entering
the glowing doorway, walking into the arms
of loved ones on the other side,
whatever your personal style of dying is.

Allow yourself to lift
out of your body, to let go,
and focus on the sound of floating
in water. Ease into the loss
of feeling in your limbs
as they become the swish
gently lapping around your ears.
Welcome the elation that will arise
as you drift through
your chosen channel.

There must be someone present in the room to call your name,
or squeeze your hand. There must be something you forgot to say
to someone you didn't realize you loved until now.
There must be somewhere you always meant to go,
and one thing you never held in your hands.
These too, will act as a weight
to pull you back into your body.

Notice the ticking of the clock, the footsteps on the linoleum,
the chattering of neighboring voices, the music playing in the
    background.
Tune in to the faint pulse of these sounds, how they build up
to become the earth singing your name.

To assure yourself that this is reality,
start counting. When you get to the number
that equals your age,
open your eyes.

Another Poem Lives

He picked me up
at the Louis Armstrong Airport
followed by a failed attempt
at the Drive-Thru Daiquiri Shop
with the joint surrounded
by 6 cop cars, and the worker
being walked out in handcuffs.
Sans daquiris, he drove me around
the Lower Garden District, pointing out shotgun
houses and Antebellum witches' mansions,
the colors and shapes, a gallery of streets,
and then an evening walk down Magazine
to the neighborhood Vietnamese place
under a vampire sky.
Now, here we are,
in his New Orleans living room,
drinking vodka & sodas out of famous glasses
etched in New Orleans architecture.
Three years gone and Little Walter
playing against the rock 'n roll hum
of the window cooler and overhead fan.
He tells me stories of his after-hours
adventures in his new adapted dialect,
with all traces of California gone.
He remains a poem
wrapped up in life.
Even his street is named after
the Greek muse of lyrical poetry,
for god's sake.

He refills our drinks
and somehow
she comes up—

Julie Valin

he loved her,
he admits.
He still loves her.

"At least you got some damn good material," I offer.
"Yeah," he exhales in sort of a laugh,
"that material can sure keep me warm
in the middle of the night . . .

if I set it
on fire."

The famous glass he's holding,
sweats like tears running down
on what will now become
this famous August night,
the humid air
choking and glistening
with truth,
as the Blues
ring out
and another poem
lives and breathes.

Like a Meteorite

When you know love
is going to be there
the next day, as reliable
as the electricity bill,
or the sun,
you begin to wish for
a meteorite
to slam thru
your window
at 2:23 a.m.
right in the middle
of your familiar dream
of the young stranger
who seeks you out
at a crowded party
in an unknown city
whose eyes sparkle
with curiosity and thirst,
who wants only you
and moves closer,
his arms melting
around you,
until the most brilliant light
you've ever seen, hot and golden,
grows over and around you,
beaming straight through you,
the two of you
not concerned with disappearing
into the center of it
and being zapped away
like the after-spark
of a lightning strike
on a pine top—

. . . or, hell, at this point,
I'd settle for a pebble
tossed at my window
at midnight
just to let me know
you're there,
and you can't wait
to come up.

Legacy

for Eddie Valin

He lived tough
and he died tough,
my uncle said.
Born at the wilted end
of the depression;
punching his way
through the be-bop
days with a cigarette pack
rolled in his sleeve;
flashing his badge #2
to bad guys wrongfully
stepping into his town;
it has come to this:
he will still shoot
the grass up
from underneath.

Julie Valin

Walker

You know how they say we choose dogs
that resemble us, as we walk
through life with leash in hand?
Walking Dead is my dog
catching a scent in the woods,
leading me around,
leash unslacked, hungry.
Episode after episode
I am transfixed
by how the main character
is going to get through another day
this time. The lengths
he will go through. How steadfast
he will be
in choosing love.
How this decision, day after day,
will gnaw away
at him, threatening to turn him
into nothing but two bulging eyes
in ugly, rotten bones.
"Look out," I call into the living
room. "There's one behind the dumpster!"
I yell. "Get him
right between the eyes!" I cheer.
The cat looks at me,
to the heart of it all,
and I realize who I'm really
cheering for.
I might as well tear my face open,
drag my left foot behind me,
and grumble, "Here I come.
Are you going to love me now?"

Alone Is When No One Notices You're Gone

If lonely means invisible
then I am a cloud
wavering by
in the shape of a hand-held mirror.

I float through my rooms,
my feet the feathers
of my cockatiel who flew
through the bars,
slowly disappearing.

The only traces of me
are white streaks on my toothbrush,
long strands
of magenta hair
on my pillow,
a few crumbs
between the cushions.

If I am a ghost
then my heart is a box of old photographs
gathering dust under the bed.

They say the reason
a spirit haunts a place
is because it is stuck, that no one
on earth or in the next realm
is requesting its presence.

So this is where I hover:
in my loft above the living,
the chatter of my family—
messages in helium balloons

Julie Valin

already popped by the time
they reach me.
I am left holding all
the little strings
that no longer connect
to any hands.

I'm Writing a Poem
ode to Father John Misty

To get to the procession
of school lunches, mowed lawns,
Tuesday garbage days
and the call of the hunger moon,
I drive.
I sing to my music,
glance at the shape of my face
in the rearview.

        I go through the tunnel of trees
        just as Father John Misty
        is singing the cemetery song.
        "Jesus Christ, girl," he sings.

I'm driving away
to where my next poem
will be delivered in the sand
by white-capped hands.

        I go through the tunnel
        of trees—dark fathers
        crouching over
        my plotted path.
        "Someone's gotta help me dig,"
        he sings.

I can already feel the weight
of the shovel in my slight hands,
all the shapes pointing
to various patches of earth.
So much digging to do.
I keep driving,
a new line branched

from my eye
in the rearview
to the yellow-dotted line.

I turn up the radio.

> *"We should let this dead guy sleep,"*
> he keeps singing.

Battle at Sea

The outline of him on the beach.
Behind him,
the waves like the arms
of a drowning man.
He doesn't notice.
The only arms that will reach him
are hers,
as she turns around
and curves into him.
The white caps are rising higher,
a looming force,
slamming into the rocks
around them.
It's no use.
Their forms are now
connected in a kiss.
The waves retreat.
It will only be
a matter of time
now.

Julie Valin

The Little Things

In the convenience store parking lot,
we pull up alongside the cloud-gray Toyota Corolla,
my window against his window.
In the backseat: laundry, toothpaste, white
tennis shoes, umbrella.
He sits behind the wheel,
enjoying not having to turn
the ignition just yet,
sucking on a red lollipop.
He takes his time enjoying it,
not having anywhere to go
or anything to do
except taste the sweet red,
taking a break now and again
by pulling the white stem out,
and then dipping it back in,
just sitting there
facing the cracked brick wall
going back and forth
from hand to mouth
like a ritual,
the wall winking with rain drops
back at him.

Wife Upstairs Crying

He tried to make it a story,
something about shadows overlapping
in the backyard and the upstairs
light on.
When he told it, I wanted to imagine it
casting an orange glow,
but I knew already
the dark had seeped in.
It was late.
The people were gathered there
in that yard, and they were weary.
The upstairs light was on
and it was the only light,
but what it held inside
was where any and all light
escaped,
and his wife
was up there crying, shadows
drifting down into the yard, longer
than the trees.
And then, I realized,
this is the point of intersection in the story
where all moments that came before
beam into one place in time,
where the shadows
begin to run over themselves,
tangled up
like so many branches,
or a broken nest.

I wish I could say
the story ended there,
when he got up, when he announced

he had to go
because his wife was upstairs
crying,
but it goes on from there
and it will never end.
That's the thing about stories—
even when they end,
the characters never stop
living them.

Chopsticks

To you, who taught me
how to eat sushi with chopsticks—
thank you.

Because of you,
I was able to eat
an entire spicy tuna roll
today while driving.
I pulled it off
expertly
using only chopsticks,
box in my lap,
knees on the wheel,
and then a Cat Power song
came on with the sound of thunder
in the background
to add to the significance.

She was singing
"I will love this love
forever . . . "—a notion
we never allowed to spill
between us
on that gray day
in my living room,
the rain shouting
against the sliding glass door
and both of us quiet
with knowing.

We were too mixed up
with everything—
the rain, the Cat Power album,

Julie Valin

the impossible
distance.

But I look back
and love how your hands,
like a surgeon's,
clasped the two sticks
deftly,
as you gently squeezed
the small, delicate heart
on your plate

before you consumed it.

It's Not a Lie if You Keep It to Yourself

I was never taught to say no.
That word was for the girls with creepy
stepfathers, or who smoked
behind buildings and wore lots of mascara.
I admired its edges, though,
when I said it silently to myself,
as one admires the sheer cliff
they are about to dive off.
So I formed it as a stone
I tumbled inside me
for so long
it became smooth
and strong,
like a diamond.
       So precious,
it was hard to give away.

And then, I finally did.
I threw it up into the black air
that engulfed it,
so I tossed it again,
which was enough
to finally hit him.
And that's all that matters—
not how loud I said it, or how powerful,
but that it broke
something.

Walking back
on the gravel road,
I rolled it around in my mouth,
and then swallowed it,
so it would scrape inside me
as a secret.

Julie Valin

The First Moment

A blind date.   The sun
illuminated everything.
I opened the slap-door of the café
and the light spilled in behind me,
until the tips of its reach
found you and the chair you were sitting in.
I don't think you looked up yet.
The sun needed to catch up to you.
You were looking down, reading the comics
in the weekend newspaper.
Then I was in front of you,
my heart a pile of leaves I raked in.
When your eyes found mine—the blue of them breezed
through me,
scattering
                    everything
all
          over
   again.

Armstrong Park with Collie

It was the beginning of a Friday night
and the end of a work week from hell.
He headed toward the music,
where it's free and open
as it always is in New Orleans.
He stopped under
the towering statue of Louis
with brass trumpet in hand,
the sun setting behind him
in streaked oil paint colors
across the Southern sky.

And all he wanted to do
was sit there, he texted me,
in the park,
with a collie.

Everything about this statement
made sense. Held true.
Except the collie part.
He hates dogs—thinks they are
man's failed attempt at being human.
I thought maybe he turned a corner,
saw the greatness that emanates from such benevolent
and all-knowing companions, thought his heart
opened a little more
to this great world.

"A collie?" I texted back.
"Coldie! I meant a coldie!"
And I could practically hear
the cap popping off the bottle,
and him laughing out loud,

Julie Valin

cursing autocorrect
as the sun set
and the jazz
played on.

Right Before He Goes

for Todd Cirillo

"Off he goes
with his perfectly unkept hope . . ."
—Pearl Jam

The California sun is out,
but there is a chill in the wind.
We walk along the last trail
and a breath gets caught
in my chest.
He notices the dead Madrones,
how they form a beautiful forest
of their own, their branches
like an art installation
of arms reaching
in all directions.
He will be going
south, and east, maybe anywhere,
and I will be right here.
We don't talk about that, though,
how life will be
in the place I will remain
with so many traces of him;
how I will go through my days
trying to gather any reminder
to build upon
before these, too, fade like his taillights
as he crosses one state line after another:
lilac, beer bottle labels,
words he said
that made me laugh, quarters
for the jukebox . . .
How impossible the task is
for the one who stays.
This isn't about love,

the romantic kind,
it's about a connection
not easily found
in the harsh every days of this world.

We walk, full of anticipation,
as if it is the day before
a limb is to be amputated—
we miss it already.

But we walk on,
enjoying it
while we still have it.

This Is Why

I.

I will miss your heart
so tender
I will love
this love forever . . .
                        —Cat Power

Forever was a long time ago
when my heart was led by
not asking any questions
and days were filled only with answers
found in $2 beers and cheap Mexican food
on Main St., or all those greasy diner breakfasts,
Sunday drives through the almond orchards
to the creek under the weeping willow,
smiles answered by other smiles
across crowded rooms, Jane's Addiction
summer parties and heartbeat bass-throbbing Primus nights
sailing the sea of long-haired boys—
so many long-night answers kiss-stitched on my skin
and replayed and bumped and scratched
on the top 40 album
of my youth's soundtrack.

Play these answers again. I want to seek them
all over again in new tunes to sing to.
My days move to slow rhythms now,
to old blues songs collecting dust in their sleeves,
and no new answers show up
even when the dependable moon
gleams its refrain in the window
both you and I look at
but only I see through.

I don't want to ask any more questions
of you
I don't want my worn heart
to have to ask
any more questions.
. . .

II.
>   *This is why*
>   *I am lyin'*
>   *when I say*
>   *I don't love you*
>   *no more.*

                    —Cat Power

This is why
I am lyin'
when I say
I am good with growing old with you
when I am not good with growing old.
Forever came too soon.
It is not tucked into the back of the pickup
that carried me through the sunny dirt roads of my youth.
It is not in the summers of popsicles and halter tops and parades,
or sun-tanned into my olive-brown skin
despite the youthful genes of my Portuguese heritage.
It is no longer in the red silk of my wedding gloves or the blue sky
that went on and on in our wedding photos,
or the late night *fuck yeahs* at a punk show
because I don't have to be up in the morning.
It is not in the hundreds of times
I played that Cat Powers song
because it brings me back
to that hopeless rainy day

when I said yes despite it all . . .

Forever is running out
on the burning legs of a dog from Hell
leaving all our yesterdays on fire.
Forever is tomorrow's answer that we carry
in tonight's dream of starlight oceans
and bottomless sangrias,
but only if we wake up
clutching
its wings
to our chests.
Only
if we wake up
still
holding
on.

The Long Night Moon

tried to finally say goodbye
to the cross-country poets
and the dark year
from behind the biggest cloud.
It didn't take.
The night is cold,
the glasses were long emptied
of their warmth,
the roads slick and windy,
but the poets are home now.
And damned if that moon
will ever leave.

Drunk Satisfaction

If two White Russians made
with your grandmother's jackass jigger glass
overtake your keto-withered body
on a Wednesday night slightly after dinnertime,
and the only person around to see it
is your best friend halfway
across the country on a screen—
are you still drunk?

We were right in the middle
of a meaningful discussion
about what poetry can,
and can't, do
for the people,
when my phone goes dead.
With that apt metaphor,
I bump around in the kitchen
with my curious dog
staring at the floor
by my feet,
and I'm doing this . . .
and I'm slicing that . . .
and the Stones come on the radio
and I'm trying to make some toast . . .
But I can't get no.
Avo-ca-do.

The knife slips,
flies and skids
across the floor
and lands right under my dog's nose,
but somehow I don't miss a beat
and continue chopping things.

Julie Valin

I make something edible
having to do with mayo
and mustard and cheese
on a low carb tortilla
with a side pile of Doritos,
because I'm a rebel like that.

I make another White Russian with my grandmother's glass,
do a silent air-cheers to all the jackasses,
and think more about poetry
and what the people want
when it comes to it.
I have no answers,
except that this sandwich thing
is rewarding
and those Doritos
really clench the deal,

which is all the
satisfaction
I'm gonna
get
on a
Wednesday.

I Go Back to the Blues

There is nothing left for me.

No one sits on porches anymore.
Only white guys play the blues.
All the old guys are dead.
Robert Johnson is dead.
Bukowski is dead.
All the poets have already said it the right way.
Every urge and impulse has been acted upon
a million different ways.
I can't even get an adequate title
let alone, a gripping last line.
Could it be the anti-depressants
are no longer working?

The good drugs are for 20-somethings.
Making out is only for those falling in love
and true love is for those younger than 40.
There are no jukeboxes in this town.
I have lost my tolerance for Jaeger shots.
No one looks twice at me.
I will never again have a one-night stand.

My best friend is gone in a different time zone,
my husband doesn't hear me
and my favorite jeans
no longer fit.

There is nothing left for me.

So I go back to the Blues,
sip my coffee
with a splash of bourbon,

watch the record spin behind the glass,
and listen to poets sing
80-year-old words
to fill me up
once again.

Liner Notes

JULIE VALIN turns songs into poems, since she is perpetually influenced by music, and she was too shy to be in a rock 'n' roll band. Her poems have appeared in *The Gasconade Review*, *The Black Shamrock*, *The Poeming Pigeon*, *Chiron Review*, *Red Fez*, and more, plus several anthologies & collections, including the *Punk Rock Chapbook Series* by Epic Rites Press. She is a book designer for her own business, Self to Shelf Publishing Services; she works at her community library; and she is also a co-founder of Six Ft. Swells Press. She loves piling books artistically on her nightstand and running through the woods knowing nothing is really chasing her. She lives in Northern California with her husband and daughter.

Liner Notes, continued

"Another Poem Lives" and "Playin' the Storm Out" were previously published in the *Gasconade Review*.

"Alone Is When No One Notices You're Gone," "Battle at Sea," and "How to Come Back From the Dead" were previously published at *Ariel Chart*.

"Armstrong Park With Collie," "Barbie (ill)Logic" and "When Ghosts Appear" have been previously published in *The Black Shamrock–First Issue*; and "Moving Target," I'm Writing a Poem" and "Legacy" appeared in *The Black Shamrock–Second Issue*.

"Empty Room Radio" was previously published in *The Poeming Pigeon: Music Edition*.

"Chopsticks" was previously published in the *Punk Rock Chapbook Series* (Epic Rites Press) and *Ted Ate America*.

"I Go Back to the Blues" was previously published in the *Punk Rock Chapbook Series* (Epic Rites Press).

Soundtrack

- Nina Simone – Do I Move You
- Koko Taylor – Voodoo Woman
- Little Walter – Key to the Highway
- Mark Lanegan – El Sol
- Luna – Hey Sister
- Built to Spill – Car
- Wilco – Jesus, etc.
- Afghan Whigs – Rebirth of the Cool
- Pink Floyd – Fearless
- The Saints – (I'm) Stranded
- Men Without Hats – Safety Dance
- Little Walter – Blues with a Feeling
- Willie Nelson – Somebody Pick up my Pieces
- Elliot Smith – Say Yes
- Junior Kimbrough – Lonesome in my Home
- Father John Misty – Hollywood Forever Cemetery
- Cat Power – Naked if I Want To
- Louis Armstrong – Summertime
- Pearl Jam – Off He Goes
- Cat Power – Good Woman
- Sylvan Esso – Rewind
- Thom Chacon – Big as the Moon
- Rolling Stones – Satisfaction
- Koko Taylor – Blues Never Die

Find this playlist on Spotify by searching "Songs for Ghosts Book Soundtrack" or by scanning the Spotify code below.

©Kate Smith

Meadowlark POETRY

Books are a way to explore, connect, and discover. Poetry incites us to observe and think in new ways, bridging our understanding of the world with our artistic need to interact with, shape, and share it with others.

Publishing poetry is our way of saying—

> *We love these words,*
> *we want to preserve them,*
> *we want to play a role in sharing them*
> *with the world.*

www.ingramcontent.com/pod-product-compliance
Lightning Source LLC
Chambersburg PA
CBHW071114120626

46546CB00003B/1333